WOUNDED ...
BUT NOT
DEAD!

Wounded ... But Not Dead!

Copyright © 2020 Rev. David Conger. All rights reserved.

No rights claimed for public domain material, all rights reserved. No parts of this publication may be reproduced, stored in any retrieval system, or transmitted in any form or by any means, electronic, mechanical, recording, or otherwise, without the prior written permission of the author. Violations may be subject to civil or criminal penalties.

Unless stated otherwise, all Scriptures are taken from the King James Version of the Holy Bible.

ISBN: 978-1-63308-607-4 (paperback)

Cover and Interior Design by *R'tor John D. Maghuyop*

1028 S Bishop Avenue, Dept. 178
Rolla, MO 65401

Printed in United States of America

Therefore said he unto them,
The harvest truly is great, but the labourers are few:
pray ye therefore the Lord of the harvest,
that he would send forth labourers into his harvest.

—LUKE 10:2 KJV

WOUNDED... BUT NOT DEAD!

Rev. David Conger

CHALFANT ECKERT
PUBLISHING

PROLOGUE

We read in the Bible that the devil (the thief) cometh not but for to steal, and to kill, and to destroy (John 10:10). He will destroy your soul if he can, but thank God that the Bible says,

> ...*Greater is he that is in you, than he that is in the world.*
> —1 John 4:4

Friend, if you are reading this book and you have been wounded in your heart by your friends or by the body of Christ, I assure you that there is a way out of your dilemma –

His name is JESUS!!!

In Love,
Reverend David Conger

There are many things in our lives we cannot understand. For example, we wonder why things happen to us. Some of them may come from not obeying what God has told us to do. Maybe God has called us to preach His Word, and we have not. Things can happen when we disobey God's Word.

I would like to share some things that God showed me in my life at an early age.

First, when I was a small boy, at the age of maybe six years old, I was stricken with Polio. I spent some time in Children's Hospital. The doctor told my parents that I would have to wear leg braces on my legs. My parents were not Christians at that time. They heard of a church south of Rolla, Missouri called Pilot Knob Church. They heard that the Pastor prayed for people and that God healed them. So, they took me to the church, and they told the Pastor of my sickness. They wanted him to pray for me.

I remember the Pastor kneeling in front of me while I was sitting on the altar. The Pastor said to me that he was going to pray for me, and that it would not hurt. The Pastor prayed as he said, and it did not hurt! I didn't feel anything, but three weeks later, I was up and running with the rest of the children! God gloriously healed my body!

See the thing of it is that God was going to use me in the ministry, and the devil tried to destroy what God had planned for my life. The Bible tells us this about Satan:

> *The thief cometh not, but for to steal, and to kill, and to destroy: I am come that they might have life, and that they might have it more abundantly.*
> —JOHN 10:10

Thank God for the Power over Satan!

I was called by God to preach His Gospel at the age of 13 years old. I preached His Gospel for a few years, then I got married. We moved to St. Louis, Missouri and I got with the wrong crowd. I laid my Bible down for a few years and that is when my troubles began.

At that time, I started a family, which I thought would last forever. Boy, was I ever wrong. This is why I am writing this book, and God told me to name it:

WOUNDED ... BUT NOT DEAD!

My first child came, and he was a beautiful boy. We named him after the Bible and his was **David** E. Conger.

The second baby was born, and we named him **Mark** L. Conger.

The third boy came along, and his name was **Timothy** D. Conger.

Three lovely boys and I was very busy trying to make a living for my family. I had a lovely family, but there was one thing that I did. I laid down my Bible, and the calling that God had placed on my life.

While I was in the dark place in my life, I would lay in my bed at night and God was with me. Some nights I would lie in my bed and wake up crying in my sleep, praying for my family.

Aren't you glad God said in Hebrews 13:5 that He would never leave us or forsake us?

And in Matthew 28:20, He tells us:

*...and, lo, I am with you always,
even unto the end of the world. Amen.*

Thank God for His Word in the Scriptures.

While in my sleep, God would show me a light in Heaven about the size of a quarter. Oh! It was so very bright! So bright that it would hurt my eyes. That light would come closer and closer and closer. The closer it would come, the brighter it would be. That big light would come from Heaven. It would hit me in the belly and splatter all over the room. I knew it was God letting me know that He was still God!

The devil would like to kill what we have, but aren't you glad that God gives life? Thank you, Jesus!

Let us get back to my marriage. That marriage was not of God. When we lost our vision of Jesus, things fell apart. My wife at the time was a bar maid. I don't have to tell you what trouble that started. I wanted desperately to go back to church. Things were falling apart, and I realized if something was not done, my marriage would be lost.

Finally, one night my wife came home early from work and fixed a great supper. Then after supper, she made a pot of coffee and said, "Let's have a cup of coffee."

I thought, *Wasn't this nice?*

So thoughtful that she said, "Dave, I would like to talk to you." She informed me that she had found someone else, and she did not love me anymore, and that she wanted to leave.

What could I say? So...she left that night and I ended up with nothing. My family was gone. My three lovely boys left later, but I was wounded very badly. Wounded … but not Dead!

Friend, if this is your case, turn it over to God as I did. He will fight your battle for you!

After this, God started showing me visions. Sometimes, God makes things happen so that we can live. This goes for man or woman. Thank God, He is with us all.

Yes, I gave my hurt to Jesus, picked up my Bible, and started preaching the Word again. I had to have something to fill my life with three wonderful boys gone. But I read in the Bible where it says:

> *...there is a friend that sticketh closer than a brother.*
> —Proverbs 18:24

He will stick closer to you than a mother, father, sister, or brother.

Brothers and sisters, if you are wounded by a bad marriage, your heart ripped out of your chest, then turn to Jesus Christ. Let Him come into your heart. He will hep you through your wounded days. You are not Dead, you are alive! Praise God!

Lift up your voice and praise Him, for all good things come from above. Do not stay in the place that you are in. Get up – start running the race that God has for you to run.

Isaiah 40:31 assures us:

> *But they that wait upon the Lord shall renew their strength; they shall mount up with wings as eagles; they shall run, and not be weary; and they shall walk, and not faint.*

Thank God that we are going to take flight one of these days. We will soar higher than any eagle has flown beyond the clouds. Praise God! Let us get up and fly together!

You may be wondering if I got married again. Yes, I did. I was still in and out with the Lord. Yes, I met a lady that was a cook in a restaurant. I thought, *Oh Boy, this is the one!*

I was married to her for a number of years. Things did not work out very well, so a divorce happened. I was very wounded again. It was partly my fault, and partly her fault, but I think God got my life together once more.

Brothers and sisters alike, when Jesus has a great work for you to do, Satan will be there to destroy what God has for you to do. We must defeat old Satan.

This is the first vision that god showed me when I came back to him: One night as I was sleeping, my spirit left my body. God took me to Heaven. I came to a huge door. It did not have a handle on it, but as I was standing at the door, it opened by its own power. I walked through the door and I saw the most glorious clouds – so pure and so white. I was standing and looking at the beauty, and it was so peaceful.

This is what God said to me, "Son, this is My glory that you will be walking in My Spirit."

I came back into my body, and as I awoke the next morning, I was rejoicing, knowing I had made it. I was alive and not Dead – wounded but still alive. Praise God!

We may walk through dark, dry places in our lives, but maybe it is a test from God to see how we are going to stand. There is victory ahead.

Another vision God showed me was that I was standing and talking to some friends. I told them that God has spoken to me to put this polka-dot dress on and I asked, "What shall I do?"

They said, "Put it on and see what will happen."

I put the dress on and all of a sudden, I was taken up in a whirlwind, and once again my spirit went out of my body. I found myself walking down a great big wide street with Jesus walking behind me. The wind was blowing very strong. Paper and trash were everywhere. As I looked to my left, I saw an archway door. Inside this door, the building was on fire, but people were walking around inside. I wanted to go help those people. It was like Jesus was reading my every thought.

This is what Jesus said to me, "Son, those people you see there have made up their minds. They are not going to serve me. You cannot reach them. They have their minds made up."

So, we passed on. As I walked down the street, I heard screaming – so much screaming! I ran to where it was coming from. There was a great hole in the ground. I knelt over the hole and put my arm down into the hole. It was so hot. I could not reach anyone.

As I woke up, I was on my hands and knees over the hole crying out to Jesus to save this lost and dying world. God spoke to me and said, "Son, you cannot reach everybody."

That night God gave me a burden for the lost. My friend, if you are reading this book and you do not know Jesus as your personal Savior, will you please make time and find Jesus and make Him your personal Savior?

God has a great ministry for me to do in my lifetime. I have walked through many, many storms, but God has brought me through them all. Just as He walks with me, He will walk with you through the storms. He will calm the storm just for you (Mark 4:35-41; Matthew 8:23-27). He will stand still for you just as He did the blind man (Mark 10:49). Praise His Holy Name!

As I was sleeping another night, I was awakened out of my sleep. I felt a pair of hands at my throat. God spoke to me as I was gasping for my breath. Jesus said, "These are the hands of Satan trying to choke you out."

I spoke and said, "You foul devil! Turn me loose!" The hands that gripped my throat so tightly left. Thank God we have power over the works of the enemy.

My friend, the devil will try to choke you out and the life you have for God. Do not be defeated! Rise up and take your place in the Body of Christ.

We are living in the last days. Satan knows his time is short (Revelation 12:12). Satan is a liar and the truth is not in him (John 8:44), but there is truth and life in Jesus Christ our Savior (John 14:6).

God showed me another vision one night as I was sleeping. I saw a great big black cloud. It was very large. As I laid and stared at the cloud, I saw fingers and a thumb on the cloud. Jesus spoke to me and said that was the hand of Satan upon the Church. As I was looking at the hand, I heard a voice under the black cloud. It was very weak in sound and the voice said, "JESUS." The voice got stronger and stronger.

Then there was another voice and it was very weak, but it, too, spoke the name of JESUS, and it got stronger and stronger. Then there were more and more voices. Every one of them got stronger and stronger. The cloud started to rise from Earth. There was such a beautiful light of all colors as the cloud lifted.

Jesus spoke to me and He said, "When my people start calling on My Name, Satan will have to take his hand off the Church, which is the Body of Christ.

Because there are so many things that have wounded us in our walk with the Lord Jesus Christ, it is up to you and me to get up and start calling on Jesus' Name, and that dark cloud that is over us and that is over others will have to lift. We are the Body of Christ.

The Lord also showed me a vision of Noah's Ark. It was so beautiful. It flowed over my head about treetop high. The Ark was restored so beautifully. The Lord said that He was going to restore the Body of Christ. You and I friend, can be part of the restoration.

Jesus also spoke to me and said that He wants to do the impossible things. We are serving a miracle-working God (Psalm 77:14). He can do what no man can do (Luke 18:27). When our backs are against the wall, then Jesus says, "Now, I will show you what I can do." Praise God!

> *For we wrestle not against flesh and blood,*
> *but against principalities, against powers,*
> *against the rulers of the darkness*
> *of this world, against spiritual*
> *wickedness in high places.*
> —EPHESIANS 6:12

We may be wounded by Satan and the things of this world, but the Bible tells us

> *I press toward the mark for the prize of the high calling of God in Christ Jesus.*
> —Philippians 3:14

The Bible also tells us we are overcomers:

> *And they overcame him by the blood of the Lamb, and by the word of their testimony; and they loved not their lives unto the death.*
> —Revelation 12:11

Thank God that He has anointed me to preach His Word and pray for the sick.

We are in now well into the 21st century, and I believe we will see God's power greater than we have ever seen it in our lifetimes. Thank God for His power. It is so real!

The Word says that in the last days, there will be wars and rumors of wars (Matthew 24:6). Surely, these things are happening. God's Word is being fulfilled every day that we live.

Sin and crime are in every nation. Look at foreign countries. Saddam Hussein killed thousands of people. He was hanged for his crimes. So many babies are killed while still in their mothers' wombs. Laws have been passed in some states allowing doctors to kill babies after they are born. What is this world coming to? God help this wicked nation!

My friend, God has a plan for your life. The devil will wound you if he can. Although he may wound us, he cannot kill us. We have the power to get up and shake ourselves off and go again. There is victory in Jesus. Church, let us pull together and get this job done!

We may be wounded, but we are not Dead!

As I have shared with you some parts of my life, I surely hope this book will help you in your walk with Jesus Christ. We all have a work to do for Jesus. Let us all call on His Name together. Make our voices count for Jesus, for He is coming soon! (Revelation 22:12)

You may have been hurt by a bad marriage or by a loved one or maybe even someone in the Church, but don't sit down and do nothing. This is why God asked me to write this book:

WOUNDED ... BUT NOT DEAD!

In closing, now I have a wonderful wife. Her name is Mildred Conger and she is and has been a very good helper in my ministry. We now have our own church. God is moving greatly in this church.

Community House of Prayer

Revival Center

16885 County Road 8240

Rolla, MO 65401

(573) 465-2511

Pastors: Reverend David

and Mildred Conger

Please keep us in your prayers and may God Bless you all!

www.ingramcontent.com/pod-product-compliance
Lightning Source LLC
Chambersburg PA
CBHW050048080526
44586CB00014B/1516